WHY IS A FROG NOT A TOAD?

Discovering the Differences Between Animal Look-Alikes

To Cara, to help her as she discovers the world
—Q. L. P.

For my wife, Jil, and to my three sons, Nathan, Kyle, and Evan—I love you
—R. M.

Reviewed and endorsed by Leslie Saul, Director of the Insect Zoo, San Francisco Zoological Society, San Francisco, California, and by Teresa Prator, Zoo Curatorial Assistant, Los Angeles Zoo, Los Angeles, California

Additional drawings by Dianne O'Quinn Burke
Designed by Susan Shankin
Typeset by Melvin L. Harris

Manufactured in the United States of America

ISBN: 1-56565-028-X
Library of Congress Catalog Card Number: 92-12215

10 9 8 7 6 5 4 3 2 1

WHY IS A FROG NOT A TOAD?

Discovering the Differences Between Animal Look-Alikes

By Q. L. Pearce

Illustrated by Ron Mazellan

Lowell 🏠 House
Juvenile

Los Angeles

CONTEMPORARY BOOKS
Chicago

Why the Difference?

Hundreds of thousands of different kinds of animals live on Earth, and some of them look very much alike. It's easy to tell the difference between a lion and a tiger, or a horse and a zebra, but how can you tell the difference between a rabbit and a hare, a butterfly and a moth, or a frog and a toad? You can begin by looking at why so many different types of animal groups exist in the first place.

All animals have two things in common. First, in order to survive and grow, they need to obtain a source of energy (food) without becoming a meal for something else. Second, they must be able to reproduce. Nature has experimented with many ways of meeting these two needs. For example, some plant eaters rely on camouflage to escape their enemies. Others depend on speed or protective outer shells. Certain meat eaters have developed sharp teeth and claws to help them capture their prey. Some slower-moving hunters may capture their victims with a venomous bite or snare it in a trap (such as a web). Creatures that develop traits that help them to survive will probably reproduce and pass the successful characteristics onto their young.

Another thing that influences how animals look or act is their surroundings, or habitat. Arid deserts, steamy rain forests, and icy Arctic plains all provide opportunities for food and shelter. These habitats also put special demands on the animals that live there. In response to these demands, the animals must adapt, and there is no single perfect adaptation to a given situation. For example, to endure the icy weather of high mountaintops or Arctic tundra, most mammals in such areas have developed coats of fur and even thick layers of fat under the skin. Other mammals, as well as certain reptiles and insects, have devised methods of going into a resting state to wait out the coldest seasons.

Still other animals have different strategies. With some insects, for instance, an entire generation dies out when the weather turns cold—but not before the insects have left behind a new generation, in the form of eggs.

With all of these points to consider, it's easy to see why so many varieties of animals have developed. To make them easier to study and identify, scientists have classified animals based on the traits they have in common. First, animals are said to belong to one large group—the animal kingdom—which is divided into smaller groups. The smaller the group, the more traits that are shared by the creatures in it, and the more closely related they are. When we are observing two closely related creatures, such as the alligator and crocodile, the differences may not be obvious at first, and it is sometimes easy for us to confuse them.

So, whether they appear similar because they are closely related or because they share common ancestors, certain animals are often confused with each other. In the pages of this book, you will meet many such pairs and learn what makes every animal different and what makes each quite special. To figure out which animal is which for each pair, look at the heading at the top of the page. The first animal mentioned is on the left page, while the second animal is on the right page.

Why Is a Bee Not a Wasp?

Of the thousands of varieties of bees and wasps, none are identical. The honeybee and the yellow-jacket wasp, however, are so similar in size and body shape that they are often confused for each other. The honeybee collects plant nectar and pollen to eat. When visiting a flower, it uses a strawlike structure called a proboscis (pruh-BOSS-uss) to sip nectar. It then scrapes pollen clinging to its "furry"-looking body into small sacs on its hind legs. The body of the yellow jacket looks smoother than that of the bee. This insect also eats nectar, but it uses its chewing mouthparts to munch on fruit and other insects, too.

The yellow jacket and the honeybee both form large colonies and build special structures to protect and house their eggs and young. The nests of yellow-jacket wasps are rows of downward-facing, six-sided cells made of a papery substance. The insect produces the material by chewing wood or plant fibers to a pulp. The entire nest is enclosed in a papery shell. The honeybee builds its honeycomb of wax. The six-sided cells are almost on their sides, tipping up only slightly. These compartments hold not only eggs and young, but honey as well.

A "Stinging" Difference

Both the honeybee and the wasp kill their prey by stinging. The wasp's straight stinger may be used over and over without harm to its owner. That is not the case for the bee. After the bee has attacked certain enemies with its barbed stinger, both the stinger and portions of the bee's insides are pulled away from the bee. The bee may force the enemy to leave, but it pays with its own life.

bee stinger   *wasp stinger*

Why Is an Alligator Not a Crocodile?

One simple way to tell an alligator from a crocodile is by the animal's location. Alligators live mainly in the lakes, rivers, and swamps of two areas—the southern United States and China's Yangtze River valley. Although they might be found in slightly brackish (salty) water near a coastline, they prefer fresh water. Crocodiles usually live in the warm, freshwater rivers and lakes of Africa, Asia, Australia, and the Americas, but some species will readily take to saltier water. So, if you see a large, armored reptile swimming in the sea, it is most likely a crocodile that has temporarily left its river home.

Alligators and crocodiles are the largest living reptiles on Earth. The crocodile takes the record, with the huge estuarine (ESS-chuh-wuh-reen) crocodile reaching 20 feet or more in length from nose to tail. The largest alligator, the American alligator, grows to about 15 feet in length.

A Closer Look (but Not Too Close!)

The range of the crocodile and the alligator overlap in southern Florida. There, you will need another clue to tell them apart, and the creatures' snouts will give you a hint.

alligator

crocodile

- wide, rounded snout
- the cone-shaped teeth of the lower jaw are not visible when the mouth is shut

- longer, more tapered snout
- the fourth tooth on either side of the animal's lower jaw overlaps the upper jaw and is visible when the mouth is shut

Why Is a Coyote Not a Wolf?

The wolf and coyote can easily be confused. In fact, the first European to visit the American West called the coyote the "prairie wolf," and the Navaho Indian word for the wolf is *ma' ii tosh*, or "big coyote"! But there are many differences between these two animals. The wolf is much larger than the coyote. Its ears and paws are noticeably larger, while the coyote's snout is longer and more pointed. What the coyote lacks in size, it makes up in speed. It can sprint 43 miles per hour, making it the fastest land animal in North America. The wolf trots more slowly, but it can run much longer than the coyote can. It can travel 40 miles or more without stopping! Wolves live and hunt together in family packs of 10 to 15 individuals or more. By cooperating in the hunt, a wolf pack is able to capture such large prey as moose and mountain sheep. By contrast, coyotes generally hunt alone or in pairs, and they live in small family clans of 4 to 8 individuals.

Measure the Difference

If you could see a wolf and a coyote side by side (which very rarely occurs in the wild),
you'd see the most obvious difference between the animals: their size.

wolf

coyote

- 6½ feet long overall
- 2 to 3 feet tall at the shoulder
- adult male weighs up to 165 pounds

- 4 feet long overall
- 1½ to 2 feet tall at the shoulder
- adult male weighs up to 60 pounds

Why Is a Duck
Not a Goose?

Can you make a sound like a duck? It's easy to imitate this bird's funny *quack quack*. The *honk* of the goose is very different. Even with your eyes closed, you can distinguish between a duck and a goose by the sounds they make. But there are more ways of telling ducks and geese apart, even though no rule works for all of them.

A duck has a shorter neck and a flatter, more streamlined body than a goose. Because its legs are also a little further back under its body, the duck waddles comically when it is on land. A male duck (or drake) is more colorful than a female.

The goose has a fairly long neck and legs. The male goose (or gander) and the female are similarly colored. Geese, like ducks, often take to the water, especially for safety, but they are rather graceful on land and spend much of their time onshore, where they feed on land plants and seeds.

Most ducks feed in water. Some actually dive underwater to capture fish. Dabbling, or surface-feeding, ducks swim in shallow water. To feed on aquatic plants, these ducks simply tip their bodies so that their heads are under the water and their tails are above it.

All Beaks Are Not Alike

One way to tell a duck and goose apart is by their beaks. The goose has a short, heavy, tapered beak. A slight gap at each side exposes ridges, or serrations, on the bill that help the animal to cut up vegetation. The beak of a plant-eating duck (such as a canvasback) is broad and flat for gathering water plants. Diving ducks that eat fish (such as the merganser) often have slender beaks with hooked tips.

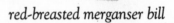

goose bill   *canvasback bill*   *red-breasted merganser bill*

Why Is a Jaguar Not a Leopard?

Either of these great cats will make you see spots before your eyes! Each is camouflaged by shadowlike spots that break up the animal's outline and disguise the shape of its body.

The slender leopard is rarely more than five feet in length (not counting the tail) and 150 pounds in weight. The jaguar is larger and more heavily built. A male may be six feet in length (not counting the tail) and weigh as much as 250 pounds. The powerful jaguar is the only great cat of the Americas. It lives mainly in the rain forests of the Amazon. The leopard, however, can be found throughout most of Africa and southern Asia. It shares its range with other magnificent cats, such as the lion and the tiger.

Although it does climb, the jaguar often hunts on the ground and is an excellent swimmer, too. It counts turtles and small crocodiles among its prey, and it may even catch fish. The leopard is the most skillful climber of the great cats. It often lies in ambush in trees, waiting for prey (such as an antelope) to pass close by. Once it has captured a meal, the leopard may drag its prize into a tree and wedge the carcass between branches, safely out of the reach of other predators.

Can You "Spot" the Difference?

If you carefully study the spots of the leopard and jaguar, you will see that the patterns are different. The leopard's spots are arranged in dark rosette shapes around a plain center. The jaguar's spots are made up of a cluster of four or five large spots in a heavy ring around a small central spot. This animal also has wide rings around the end of its tail.

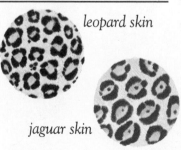

leopard skin

jaguar skin

Why Is a Frog Not a Toad?

Have you ever wondered why there are frog-jumping contests but no toad-jumping contests? Both animals are good at hopping from place to place, but frogs are the long-distance champs. (During a contest in 1970, a six-inch-long frog made a jump of more than 18 feet!) Compared to a toad's short, stocky legs, a frog's long, slender legs are better suited for leaping over great distances. There are other differences, too. A frog is usually slimmer, and its snout is more pointed than that of a chubby toad. You're likely to find frogs living near the edge of a pond, lake, or river, or in damp meadows or marshes.

Many toads live in wet or damp places, too, but some live in hot, dry deserts. Frogs and toads both lay their eggs in or near water. A desert toad must often wait until a rainstorm arrives. Then it lays its eggs in a newly formed puddle. The eggs must hatch into tadpoles and then develop into toads before the puddle disappears in the hot desert sun.

Frogs and toads make special calls to attract mates. They produce a call by forcing air from their lungs into their mouths, then expanding a throat sac to make the sound louder. Toads and tree frogs have a single throat sac, while most other frogs have a sac on each side of their mouths.

You Can Touch the Difference!

You can sometimes tell the difference between a frog and a toad just by the way they feel. The skin of a toad is rough, bumpy, and often feels dry. A frog's skin is usually smooth, and with some varieties, such as arrow-poison frogs, it can be very brightly colored.

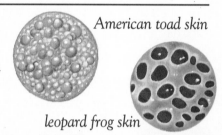

American toad skin

leopard frog skin

Why Is an Antelope Not a Deer?

Both deer and antelope come in many shapes and sizes, and they live in a wide range of similar habitats. So how can you tell them apart? As with all large groups of animals, there are exceptions, but most male and many female antelope sport a single pair of unbranched horns on their heads. Horns are hollow sheaths of material (like the material that makes up your fingernails) that cap a bony spike. Antelope do not shed their horns, and if one is lost, it is not replaced. Most male deer—and with caribou, both male and female—are crowned with solid, bony antlers. Antlers grow and are shed yearly, and if a deer loses one, it will grow back.

As we learned earlier, scientists classify animals into groups to make them easier to study. Deer make up one large family. The family that includes antelope also contains cattle, sheep, and goats. Deer are either native to or have been introduced into all of Earth's continents except Antarctica. Antelope are found only in Africa and Eurasia. Although some call the North American pronghorn an antelope, this animal actually belongs to its own separate family.

A Closer Look at Horns and Antlers

Antelope horns and deer antlers come in a variety of shapes and sizes. The horns of some antelope are small and simple, while others may twist or curl. One of the longest horns belongs to the greater kudu of Africa, whose horns are more than four feet long.

The antlers of some deer may be no more than short, twin-pronged spikes, while others are long and have many branches (called tines). The antlers of the moose (a member of the deer family) may have a spread of up to six feet wide.

red deer

giant sable

greater kudu

North American moose

Why Is a Turtle
Not (Always) a Tortoise?

The tortoise is, in fact, a variety of turtle. What mainly sets it apart from
its cousins is that it is land-dwelling. Some tortoises live on remote islands,
others in damp woodlands or arid deserts. Generally a vegetarian, the tortoise
clips plant leaves with its sharp-edged beak or digs up roots to eat. The animal
commonly called a turtle spends most or all of its life in water. It feeds on water
plants or on such animals as worms, snails, insects, fish, and shellfish.

The shell of a tortoise is high and domed. When the animal is
frightened, it usually pulls in its head and tail while drawing its scaly legs
together to close the opening over its head. A turtle's shell is
usually smooth or somewhat flattened. When
threatened, most turtles can pull their
heads, tails, and legs into
their shells.

Compare the Legs

The legs of the tortoise and the turtle are very different from each other because the tortoise lives on land, and the turtle spends much of its time in water.

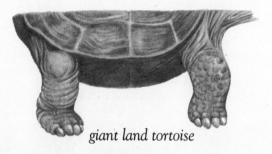

giant land tortoise

- has strong, elephantlike hind legs to move its bulk on land
- front feet have sharp claws for digging

*mud turtle
(a freshwater turtle)*

- has slender legs and wide, webbed feet because it spends much of its time in freshwater rivers, lakes, or ponds

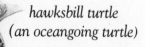

*hawksbill turtle
(an oceangoing turtle)*

- has broad, flat fins because it spends almost all of its time in water

Why Is a Rabbit
Not a Hare?

It is easy to tell the difference between rabbits and hares from the moment they are born. Baby rabbits, called kittens (or sometimes fawns), are born blind, deaf, and hairless. They need a great deal of care and protection. Baby hares, or leverets, are born open-eyed and fully furred. They are able to move about only a few hours after birth.

The hare is generally larger than the rabbit and has longer ears and legs. With its powerful hind legs, the hare can run farther, leap greater distances, and move faster than the rabbit. When frightened, the jackrabbit of the western United States (which is, in fact, a hare) may cover 15 feet in a single leap and reach speeds of up to 40 miles per hour. For this reason, the hare seems to prefer open spaces that permit a rapid getaway from predators. The slower-moving rabbit relies on hiding in dense cover or escaping down a burrow to elude its enemies.

Preparing a Home

There is a difference in the way in which hares and rabbits prepare for the birth of their young. Like many rabbits, the European rabbit builds a system of tunnels or burrows known as a warren. The young are born in an underground chamber lined with grass and fur. Some female hares dig a shallow depression in the ground and line it with fur. Other hares build no nest at all.

rabbit's burrow

hare's nest

Why Is an Ape Not a Monkey?

Monkeys and apes belong to the same major group, the Primates, which also includes humans. The monkeys found in Africa and Asia are called Old World monkeys. Their nostrils are usually very close together and face down or forward. Some have tails, others do not. Some live in the trees and some on the ground. Ground-dwelling monkeys walk with all four feet flat. The monkeys of South and Central America are called New World monkeys. Their nostrils are set farther apart and face outward. Generally small, New World monkeys all live in trees. Most are equipped with prehensile (grasping) tails.

Apes, which include chimpanzees, orangutans, and gorillas, are found only in Africa and Asia. Compared to monkeys, apes have longer forelimbs, shorter hind legs, and no tails. Gorillas and chimpanzees walk with their hind feet flat, but they curl the fingers of their hands under.

Compare Size

Perhaps the most striking difference between monkeys and apes is size. The gorilla is the largest of the great apes, and the chimpanzee is the smallest. The largest Old World monkey is the baboon. In the New World, the record goes to the howler monkey, and one of the smallest monkeys is the pygmy marmoset. Here are a few comparisons:

gorilla
6 feet
500 pounds

chimpanzee
3 feet
110 pounds

baboon
3½ feet
100 pounds

howler monkey
2 to 3 feet
20 pounds

pygmy marmoset
7 inches
3 ounces

Why Is a Butterfly Not a Moth?

Although there are exceptions to almost every rule for telling moths and butterflies apart, if you look closely you can gather several clues. For instance, both these insects have a pair of antennae(an-TEN-ee)on their heads that they use for taste, touch, and smell. But while a moth's antennae may be threadlike or feathery, those of the butterfly are often smooth, with a little knob at the end.

A moth of North America is usually patterned in soft colors of cream, gray, or brown that help the insect to blend in with its background. The moth rests during the day with its wings outstretched or folded down along its back. The butterfly is often very colorful, and it rests at night, with its delicate wings raised together above the back of its slender body.

Transformations

Both moths and butterflies develop in four stages: egg, larva (or caterpillar), pupa, and adult. To prepare for the pupal, or resting, stage, moth caterpillars burrow into the ground or under leaves, or they spin a silken cocoon around themselves. During their pupal stage, butterflies form a tough outer covering called a chrysalis(KRISS-uh-luss).

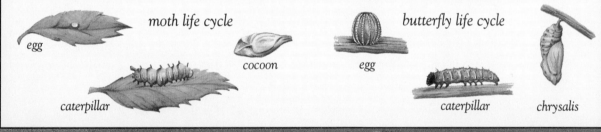

moth life cycle

egg

cocoon

caterpillar

butterfly life cycle

egg

caterpillar

chrysalis

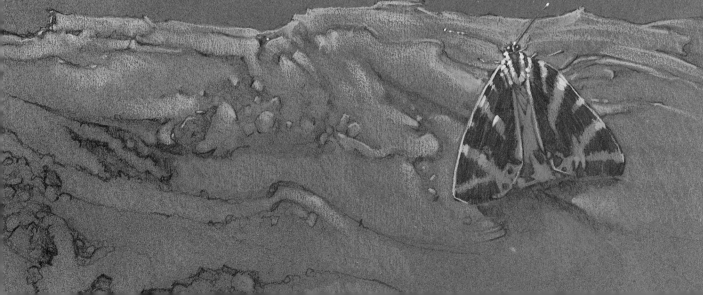

Q. L. Pearce has written more than fifty science books for children. An enthusiastic naturalist, her credits include the *Nature's Footprints*, *Giants*, and *Amazing Science* series. She and her husband live in Claremont, California.

Ron Mazellan received his B.A. in art from Wheaton College, in Wheaton, Illinois. His artwork has appeared on the covers of many adult and children's books, including *Children of the Furor*, *Victory Over the Darkness*, and the *Bradford Family Adventures* series. Ron lives with his wife and their three children in Southern California.